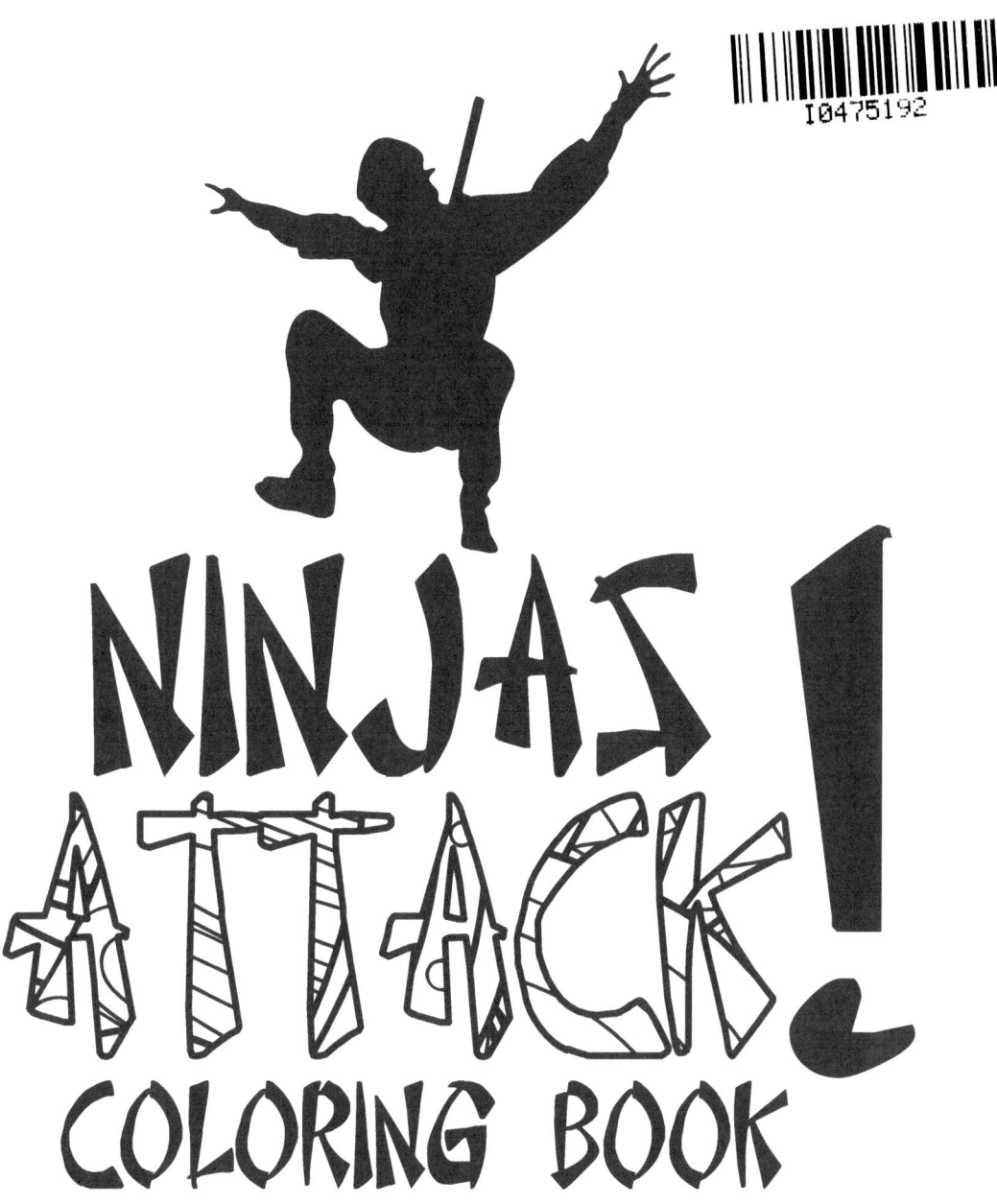

NINJAS ATTACK!
COLORING BOOK

Coloring book art by Redlands, CA artist Bruce Herwig
Follow this link for some FREE bonus coloring pages:
www.bruceherwig.wordpress.com/NinjasAttack

Feel free to copy these pages for your personal or classroom use.
Please encourage your friends to get their own copy.

"Inspired by the Zentangle® method of pattern drawing."

• COLOR AT YOUR OWN RISK •
Side effects include stress relief, mental clarity, smiles and fun!

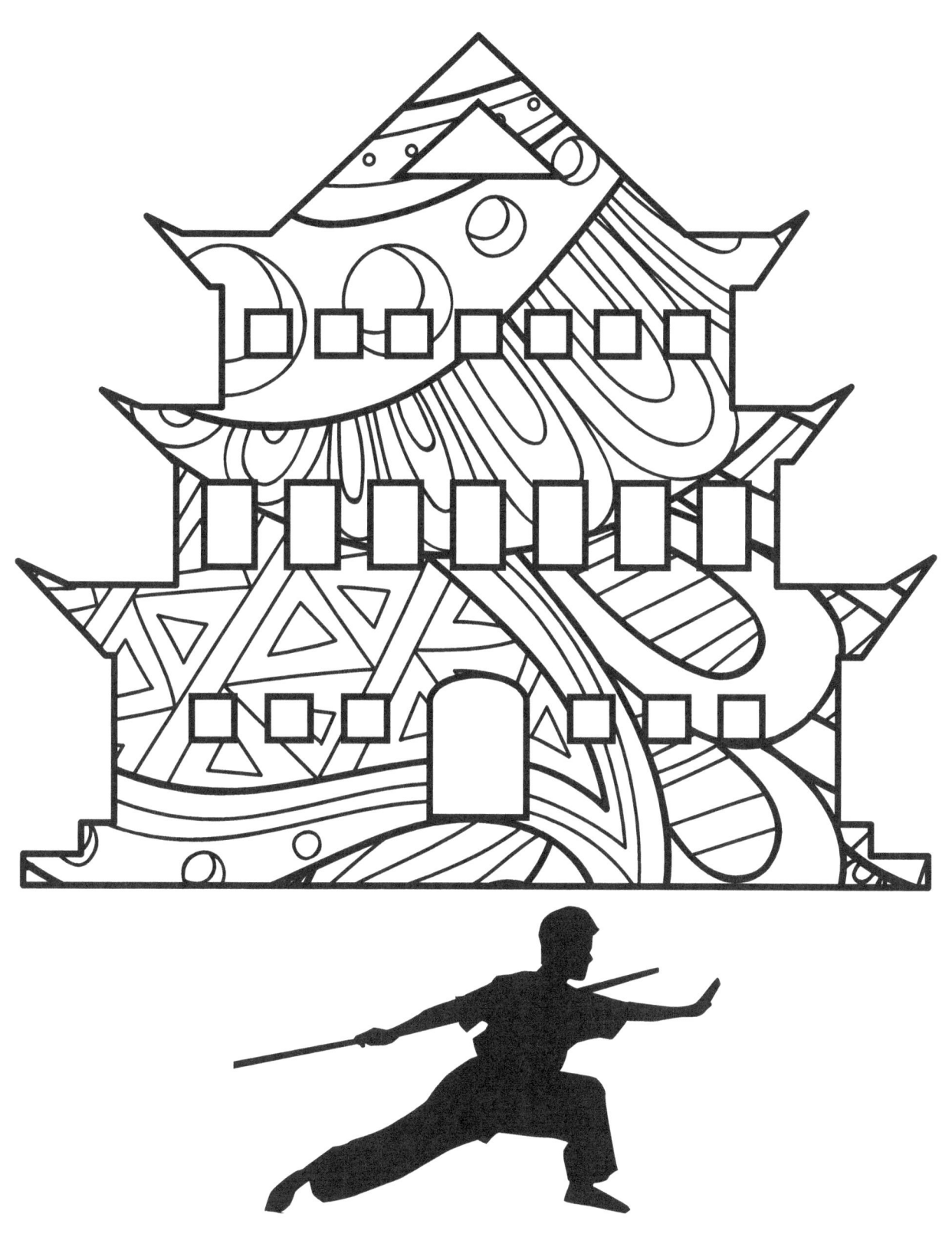

JAPAN THE LAND OF NINJAS

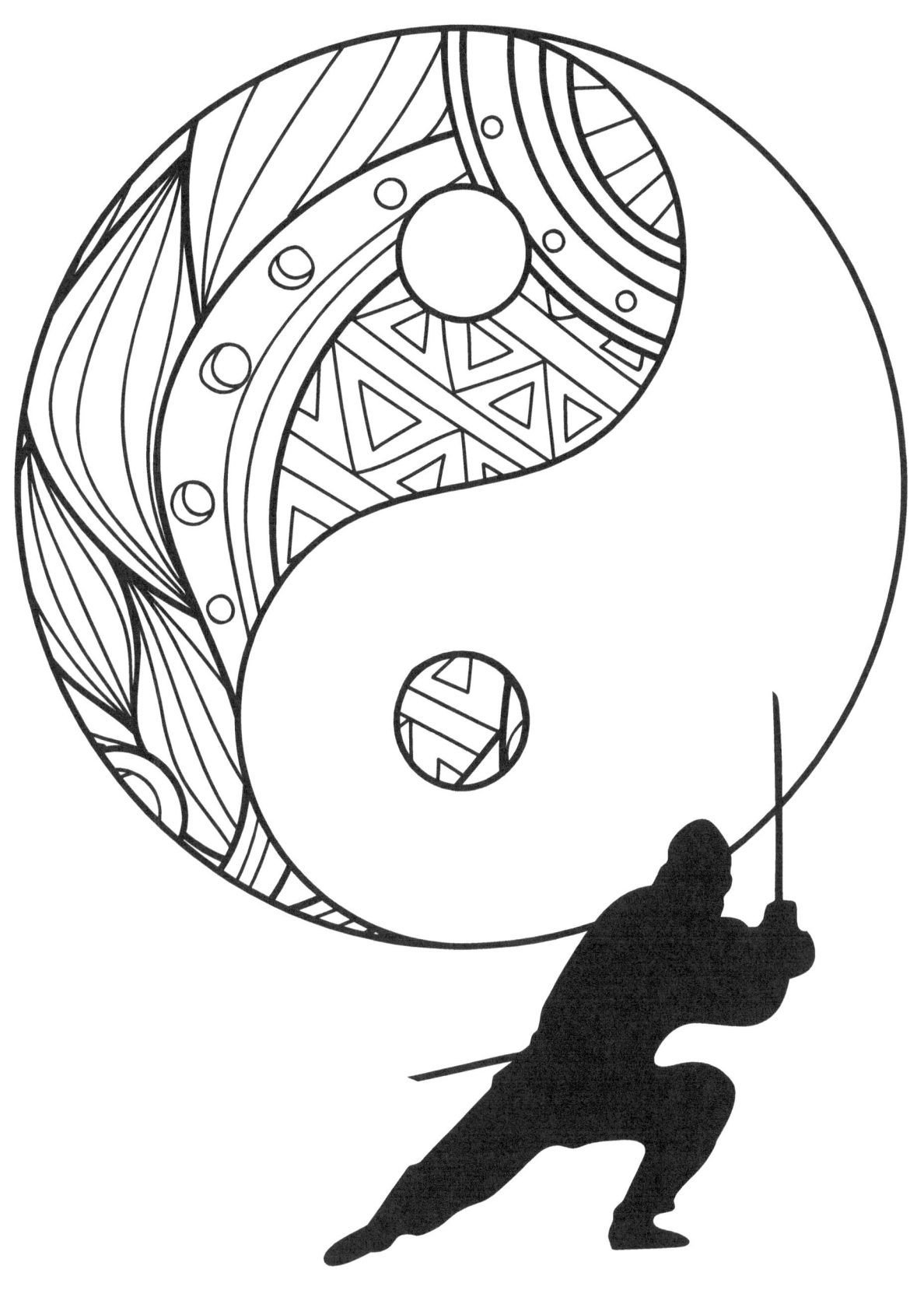

YIN AND YANG

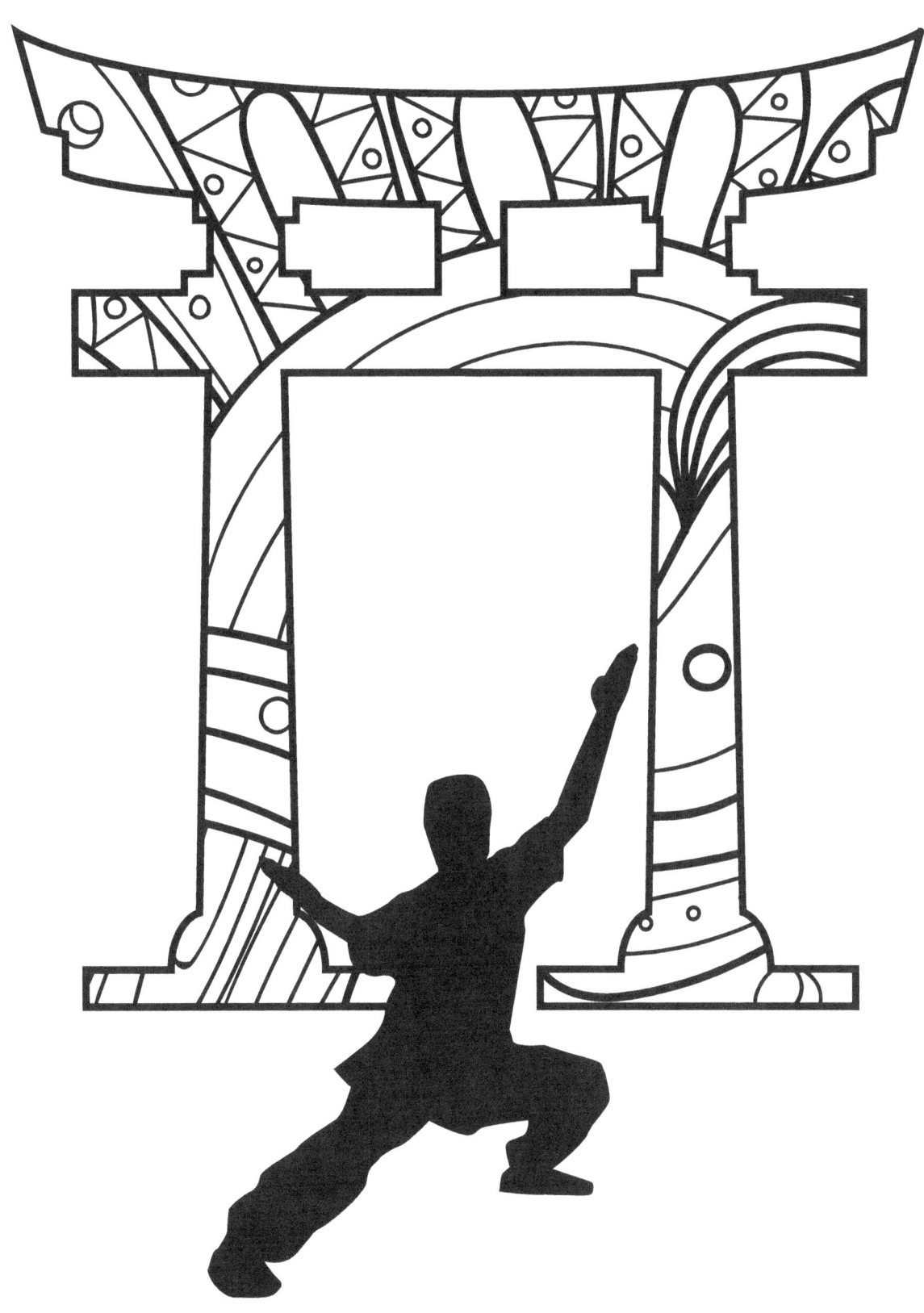

TORII GATE

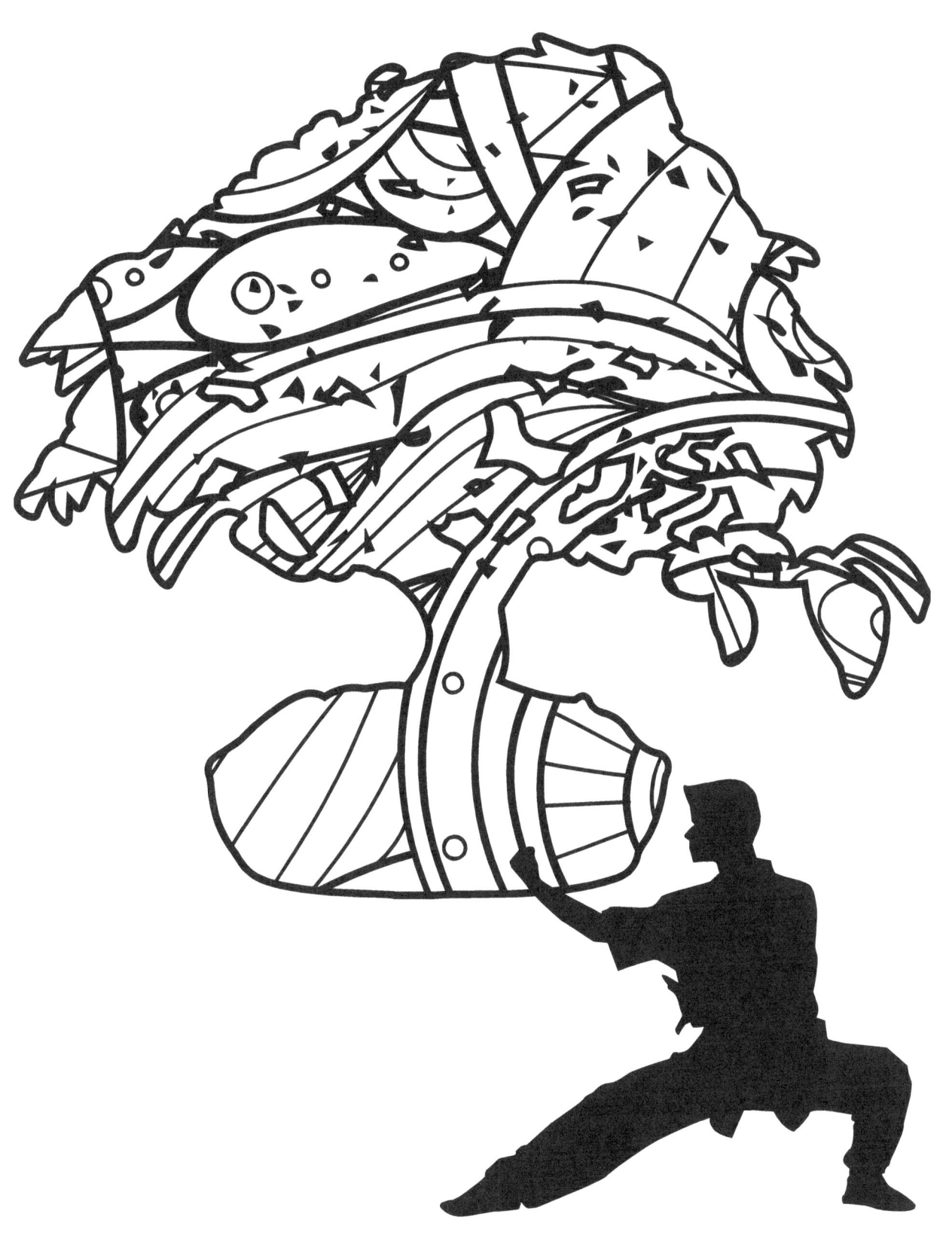

BONSAI TREE

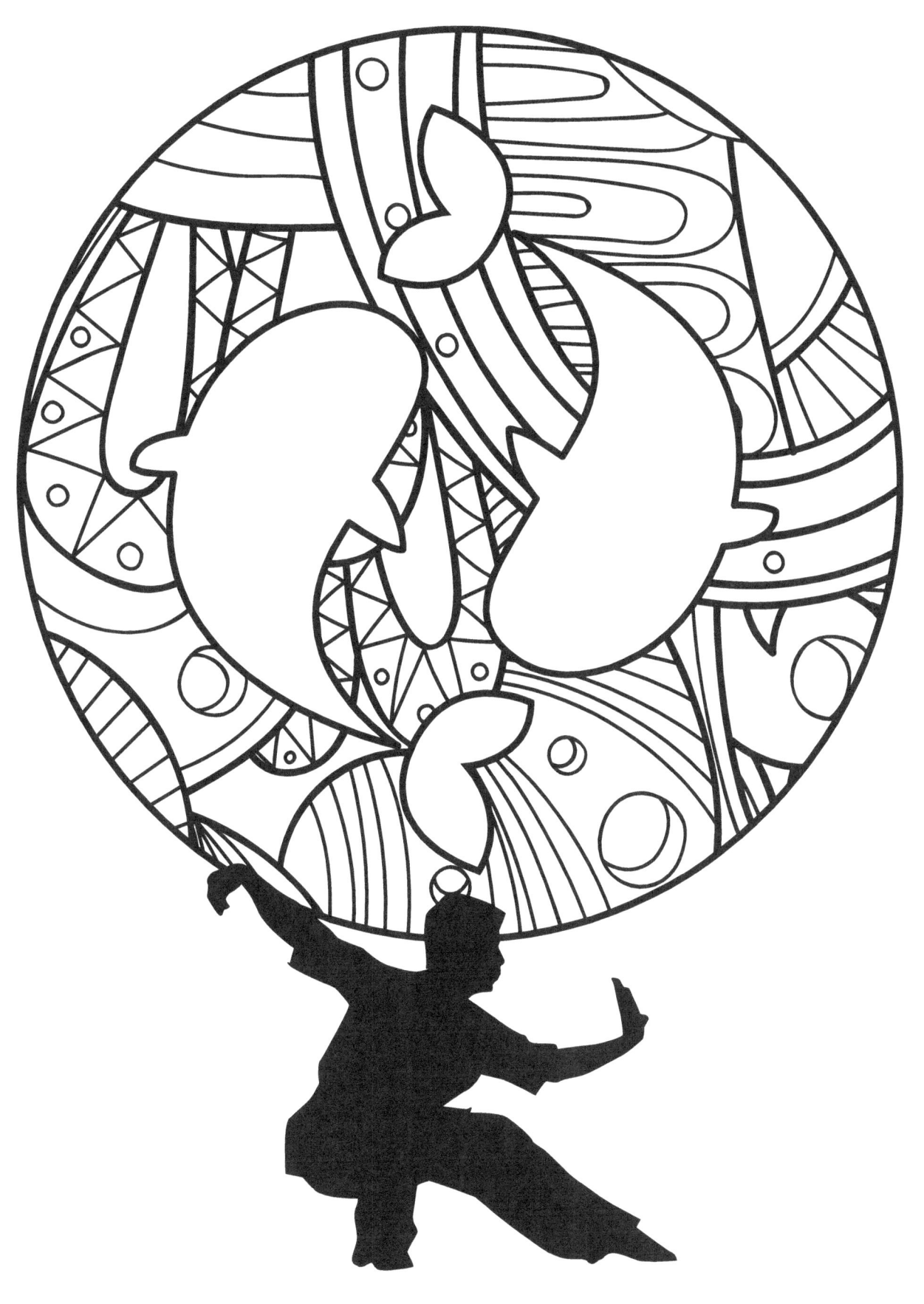

KOI FISH

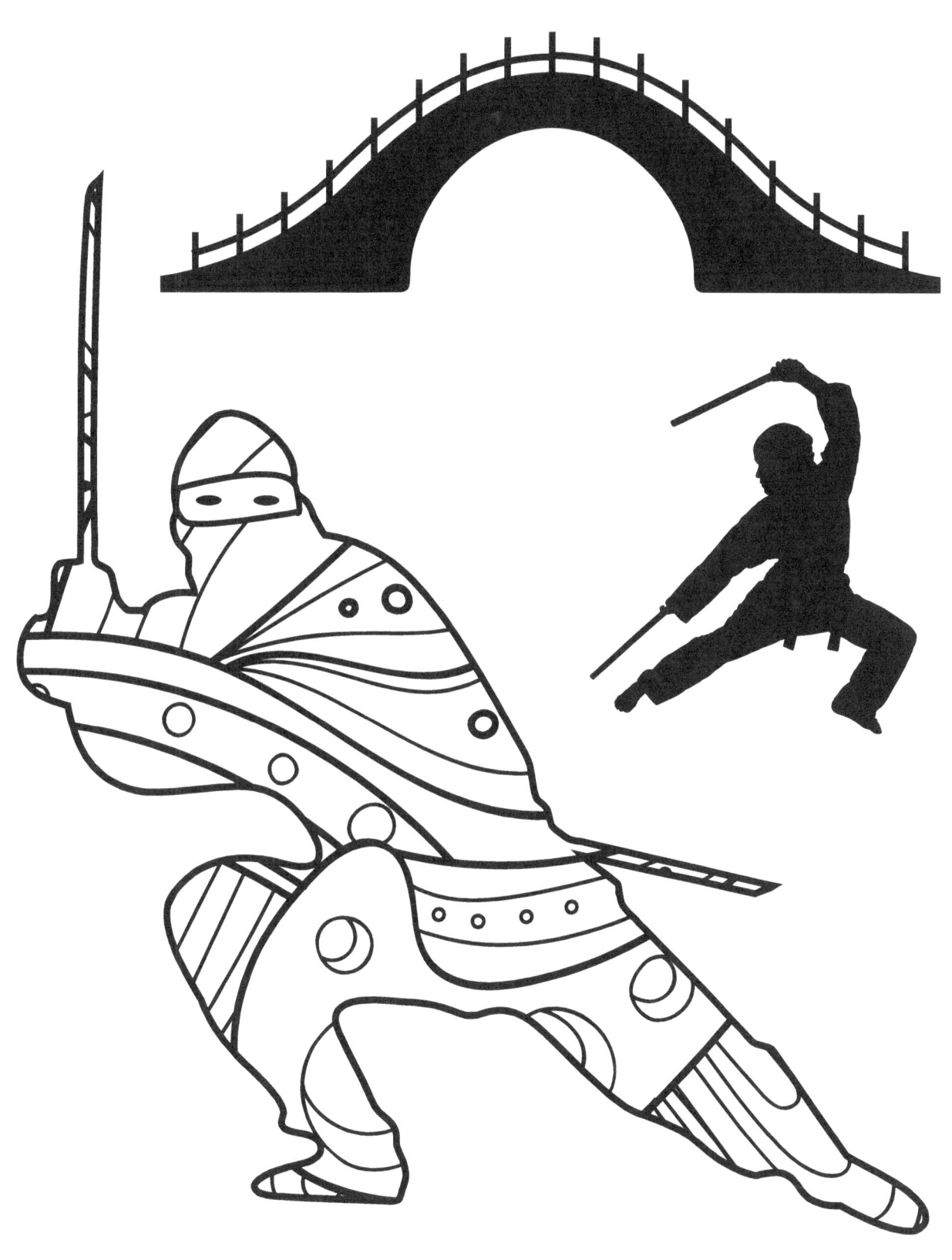

READY TO ATTACK

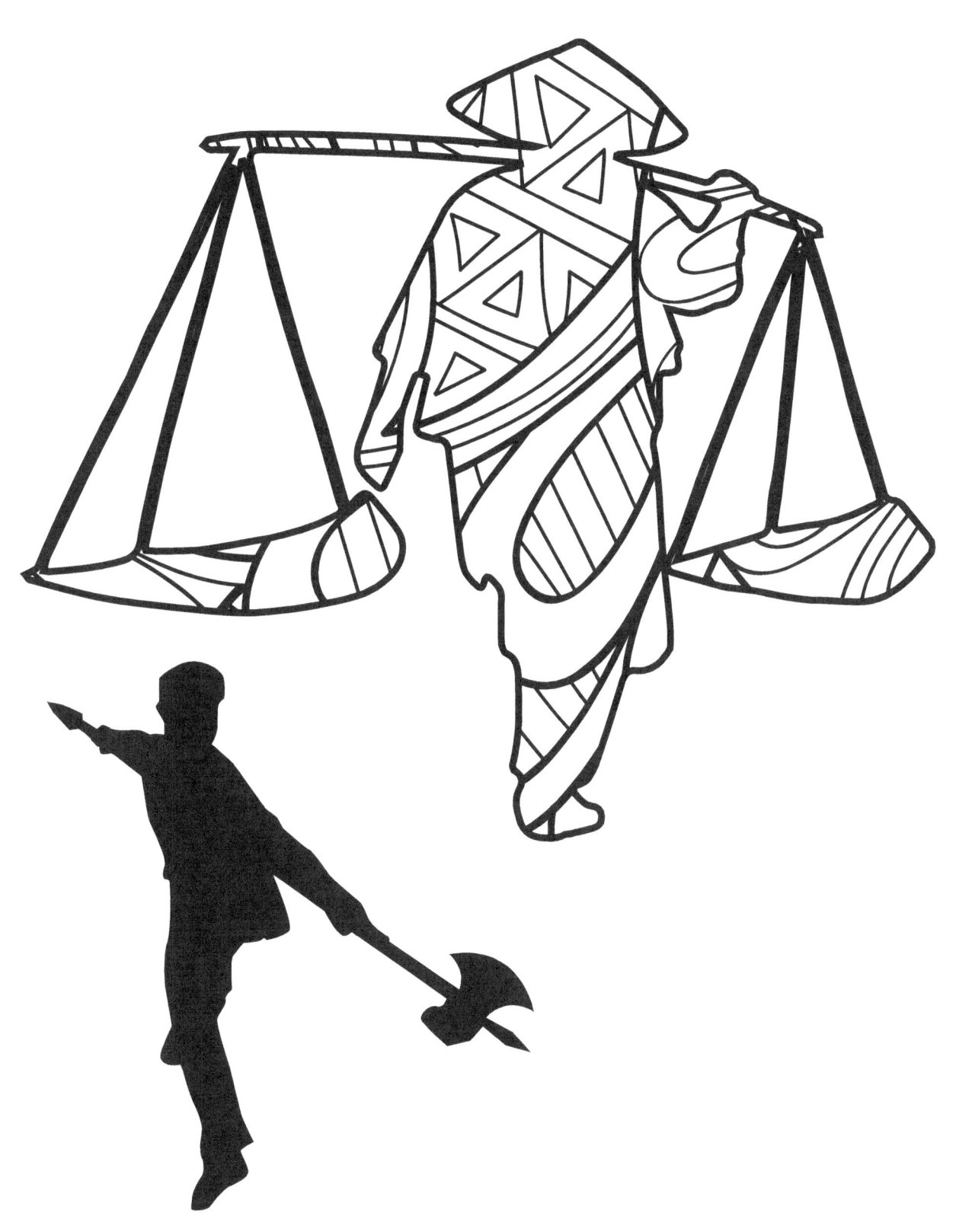

PEASANT FARMER OR NINJA SPY?

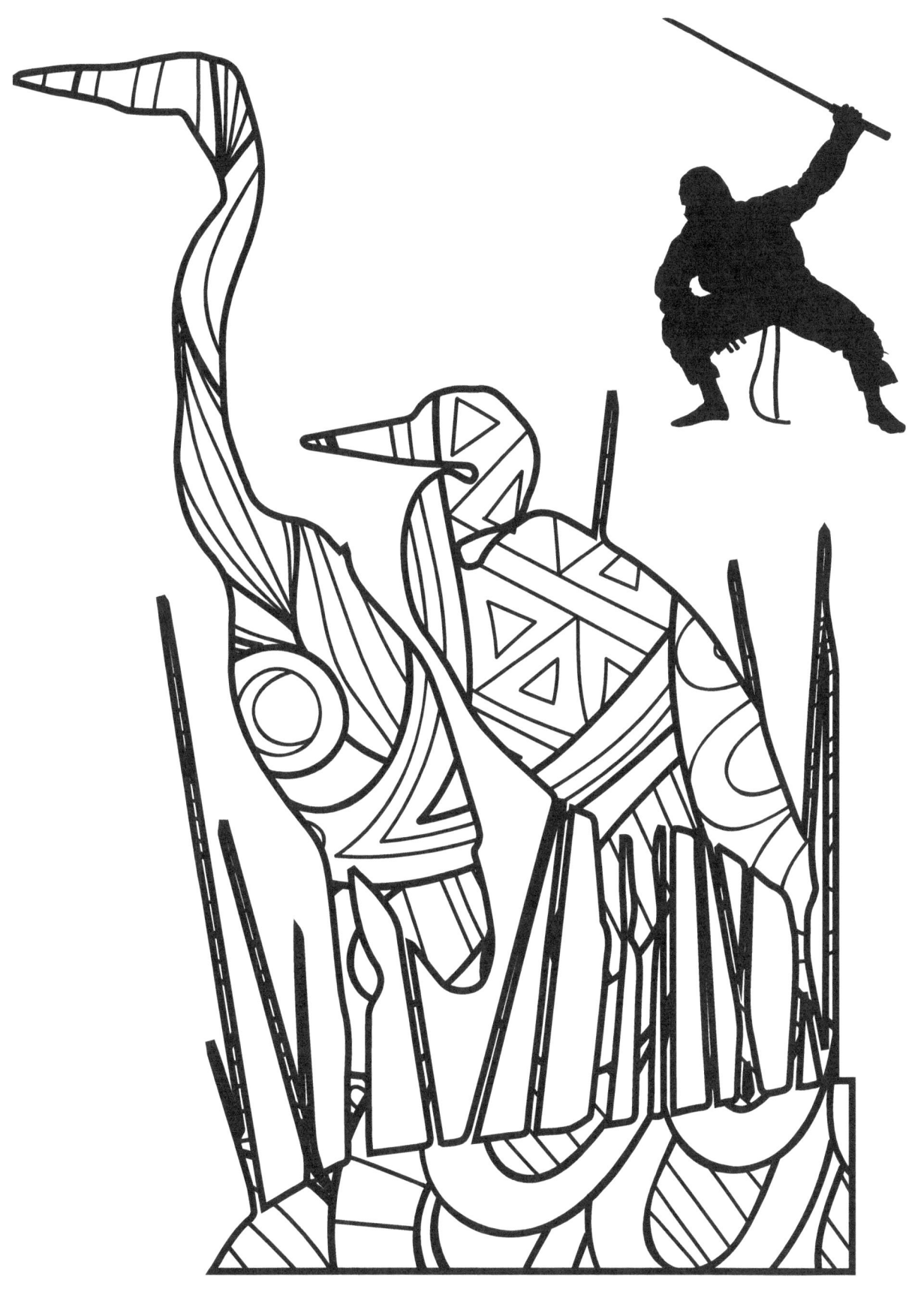

JAPANESE CRANES BRING LUCK

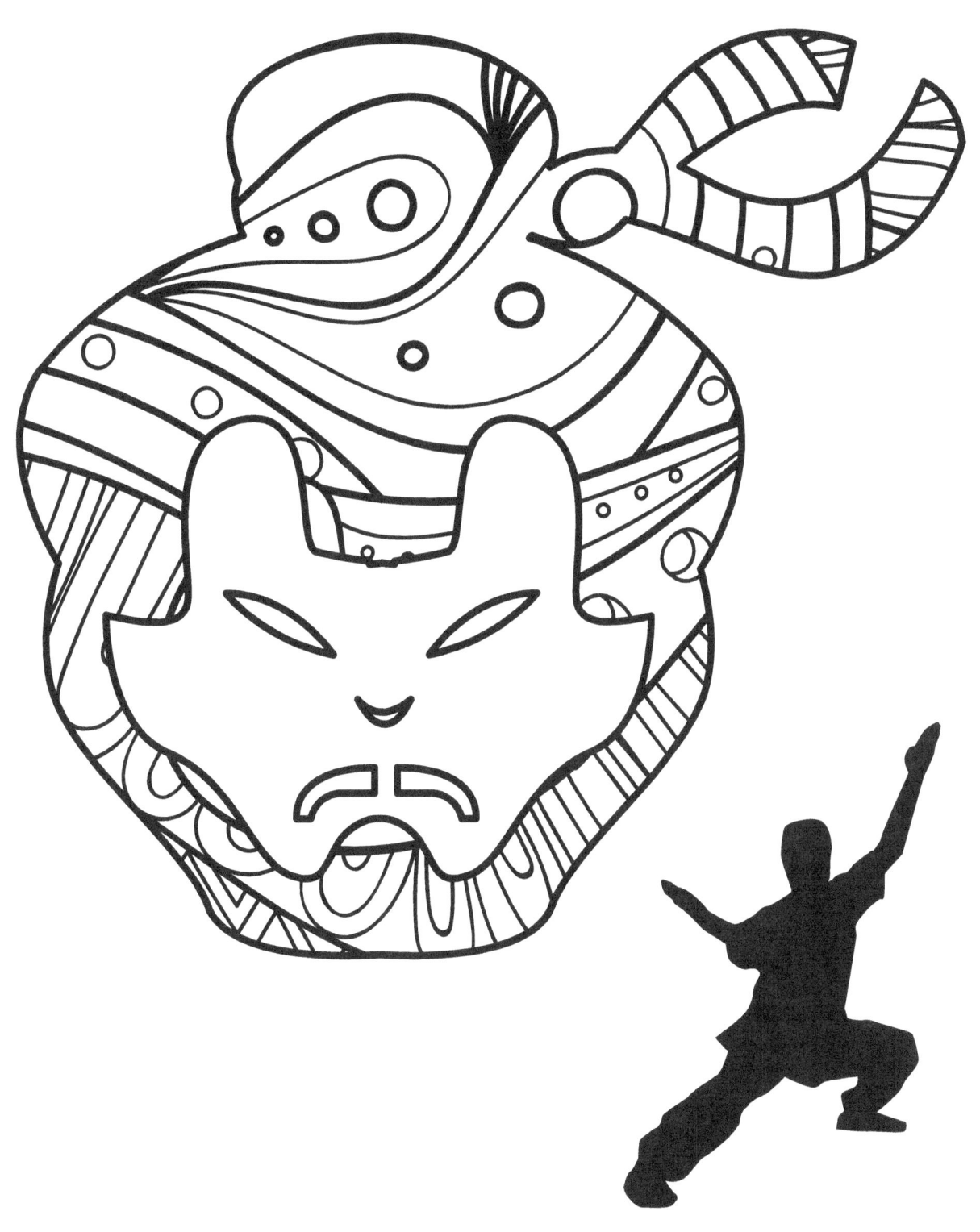

NINJA WARRIOR

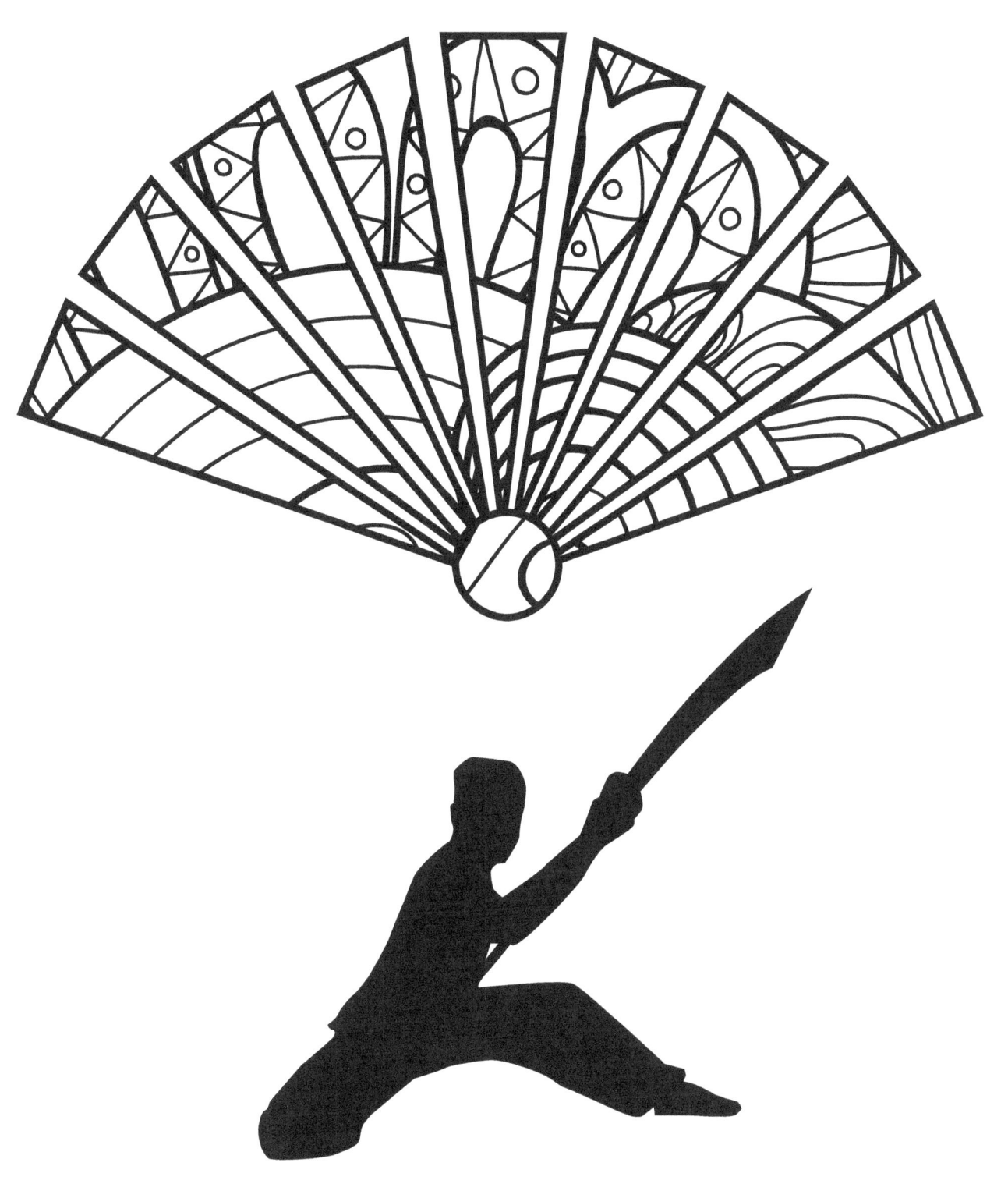

JAPANESE WAR FAN

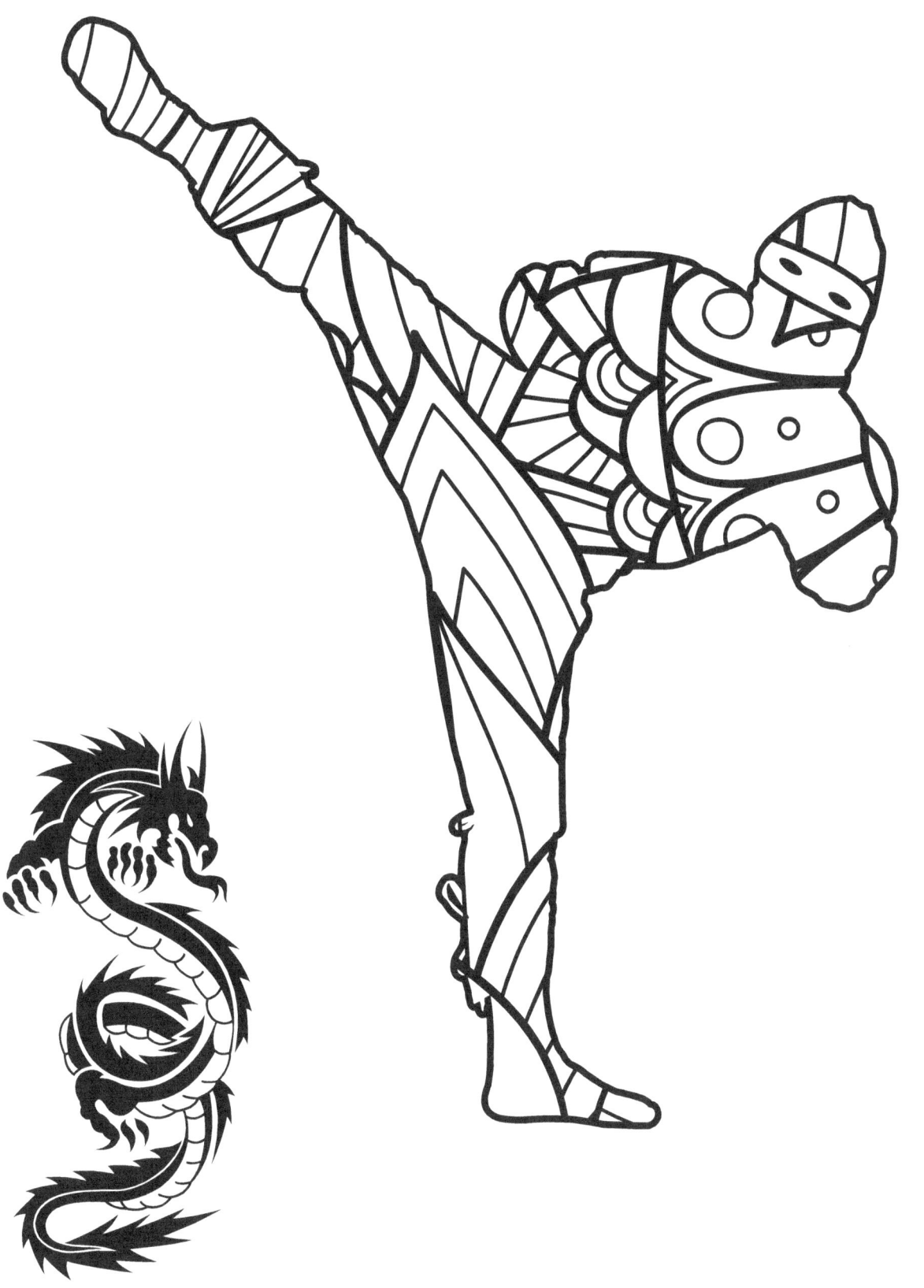

NINJA HIGH KICK

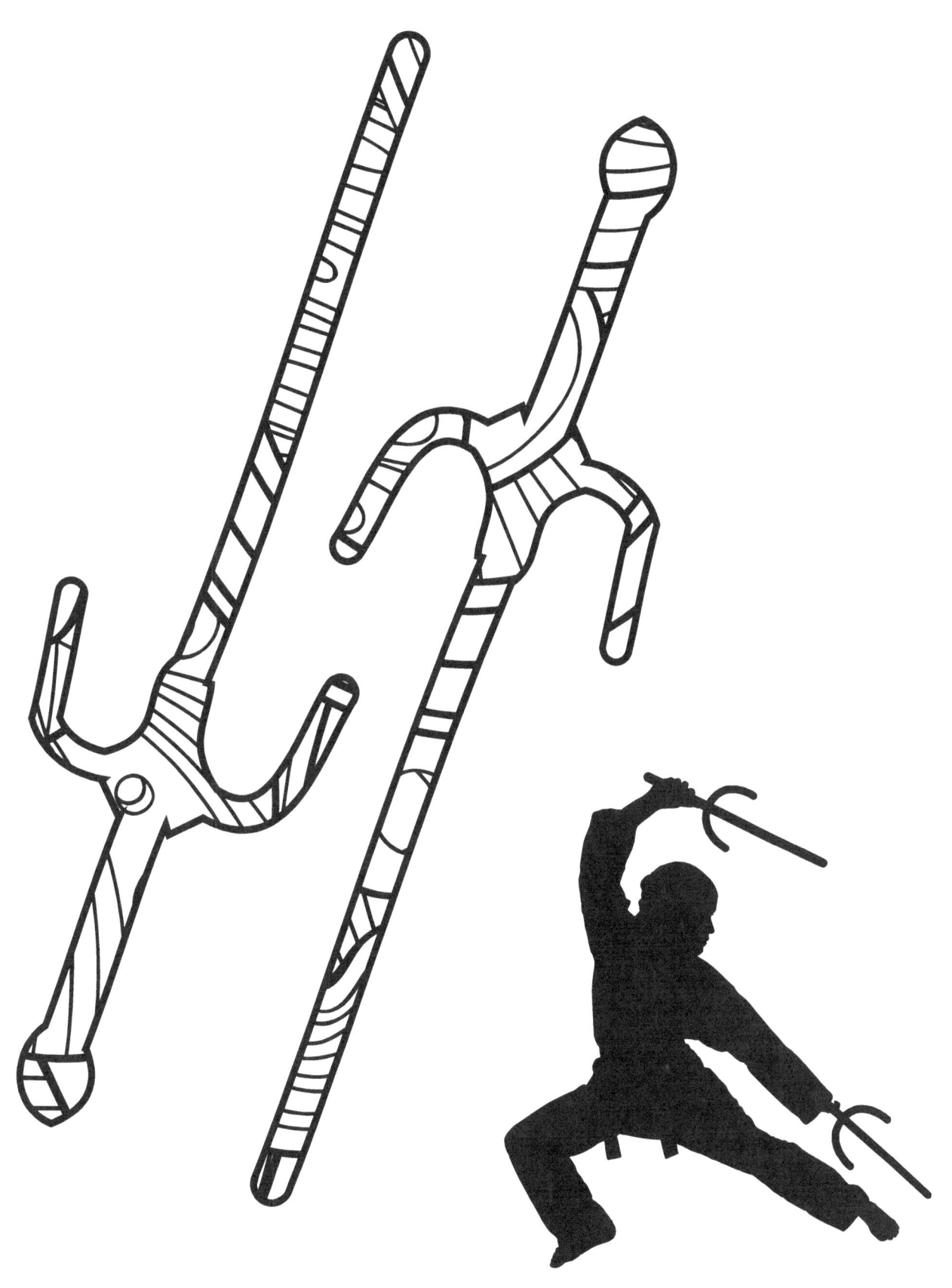

TRADITIONAL SAI WEAPONS

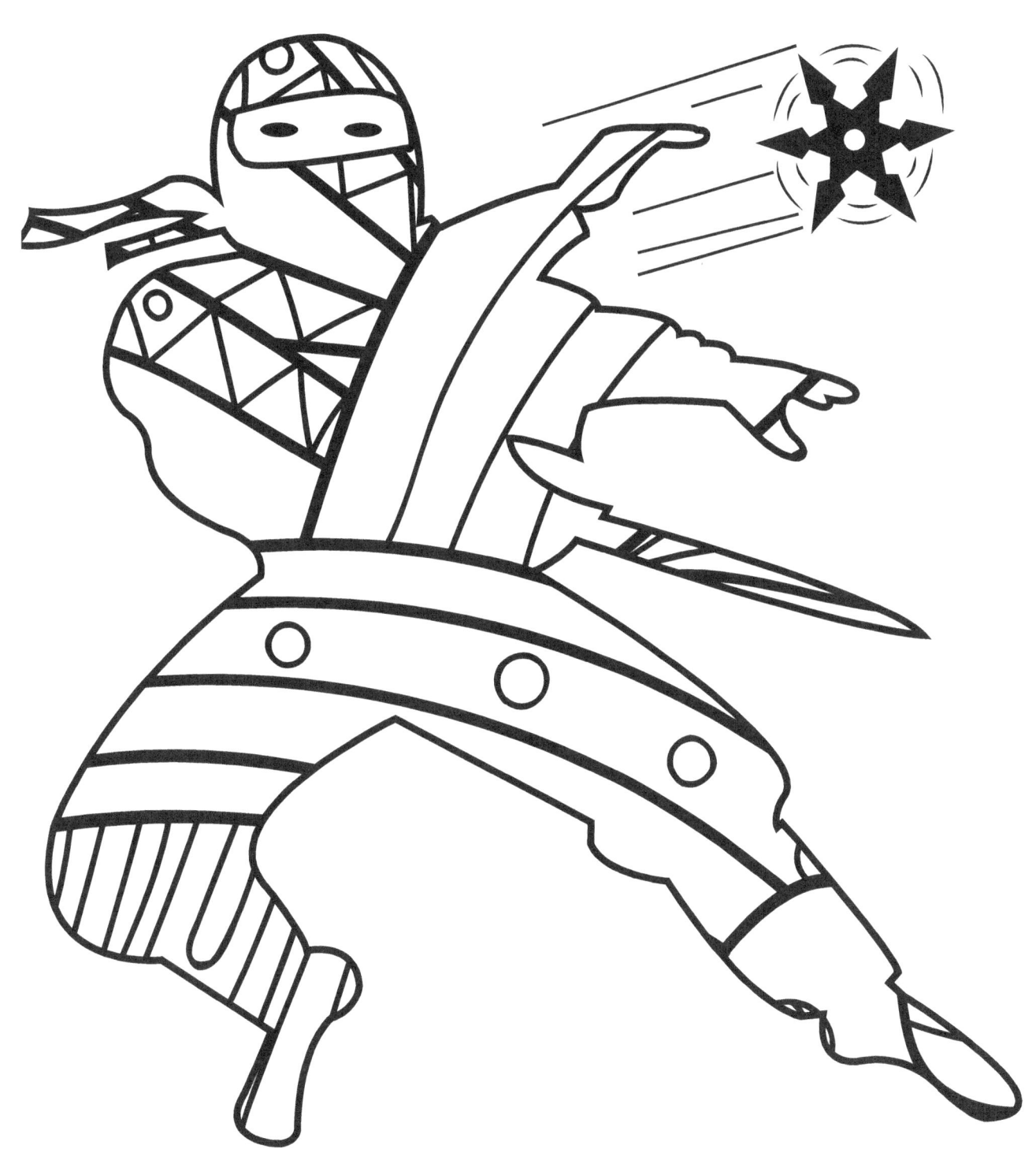

NINJA THROWING STARS

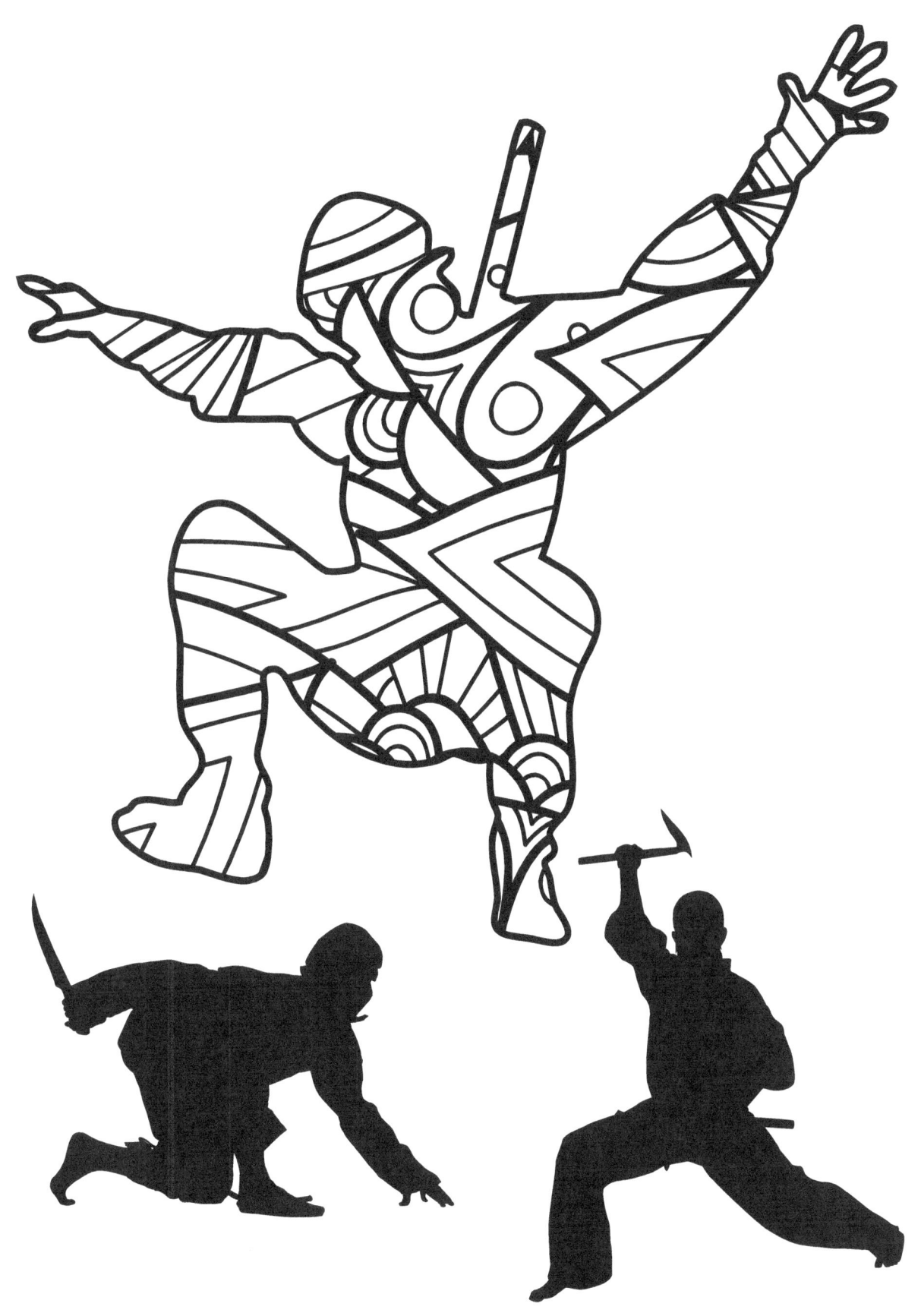

FIGHTING NINJAS

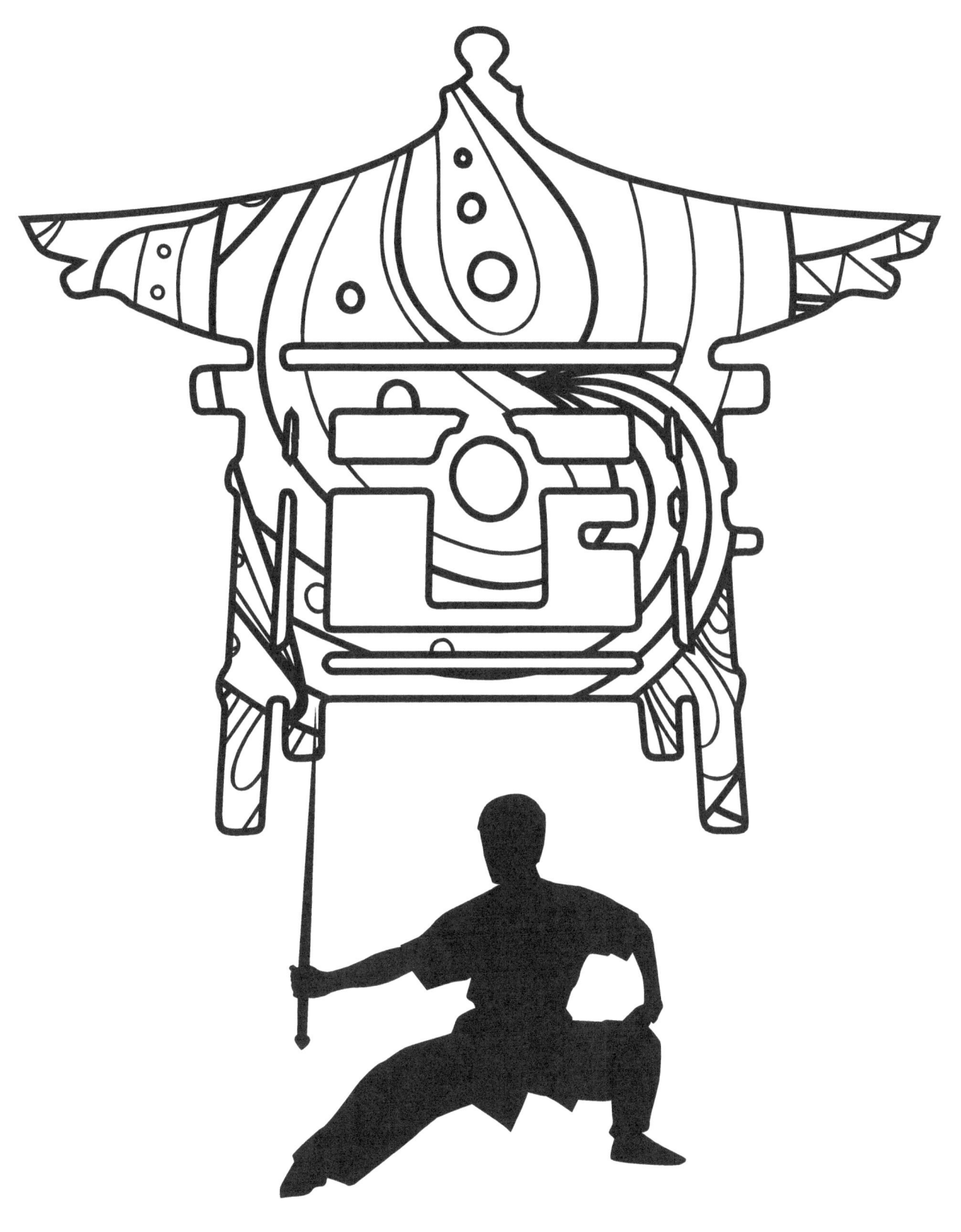

NINJA TRAINING TEMPLE

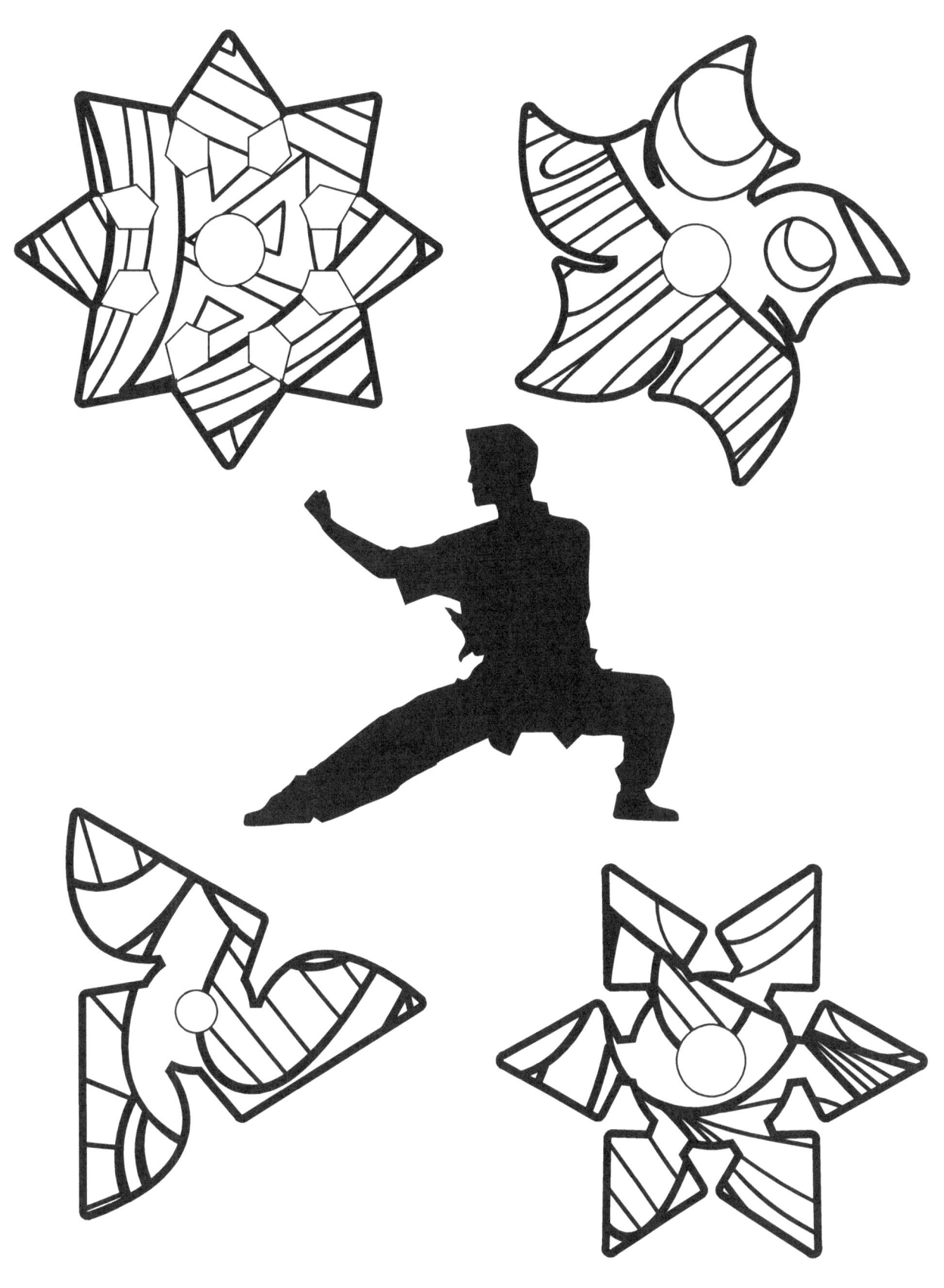

THROWING STARS

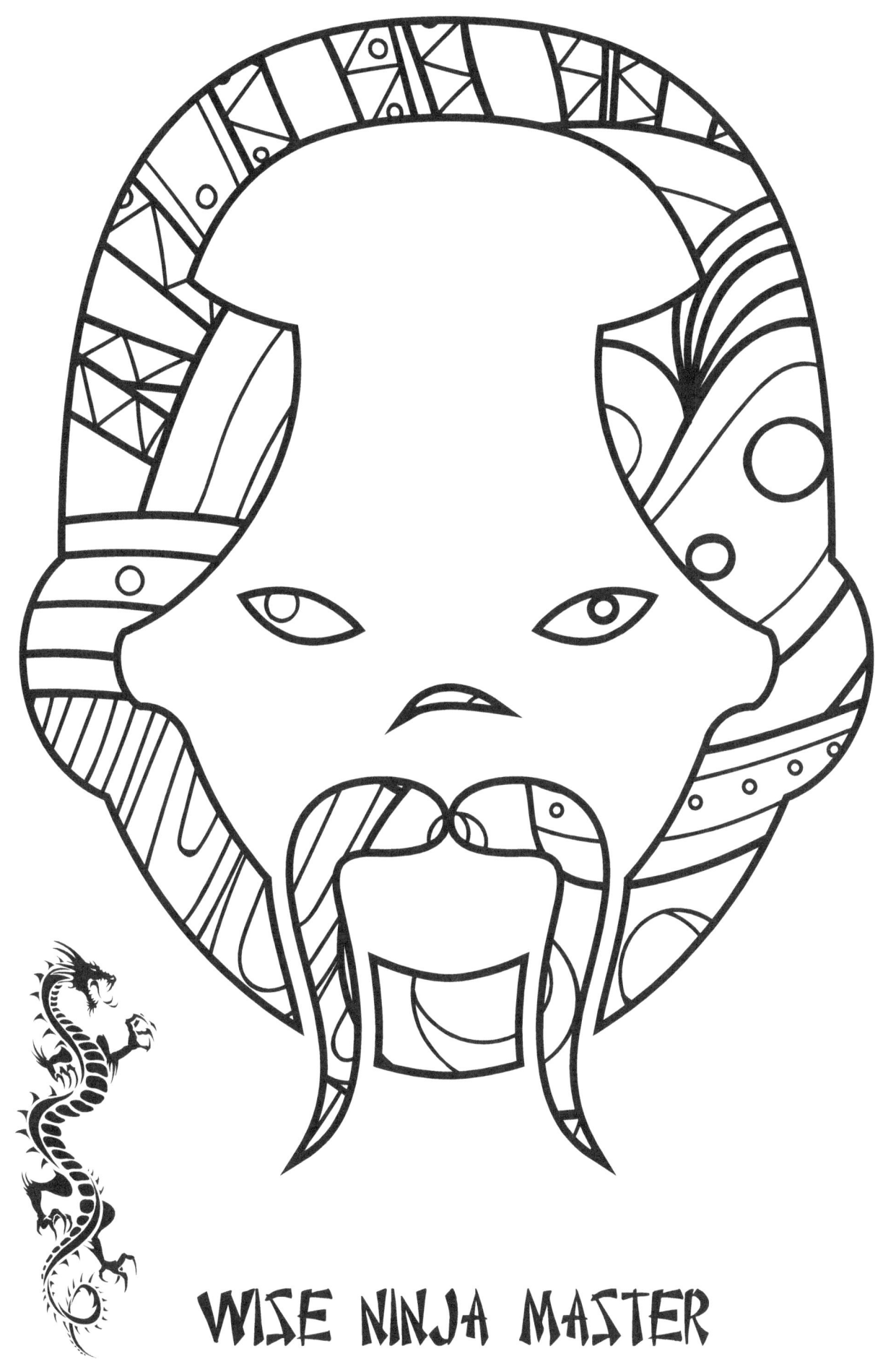

WISE NINJA MASTER

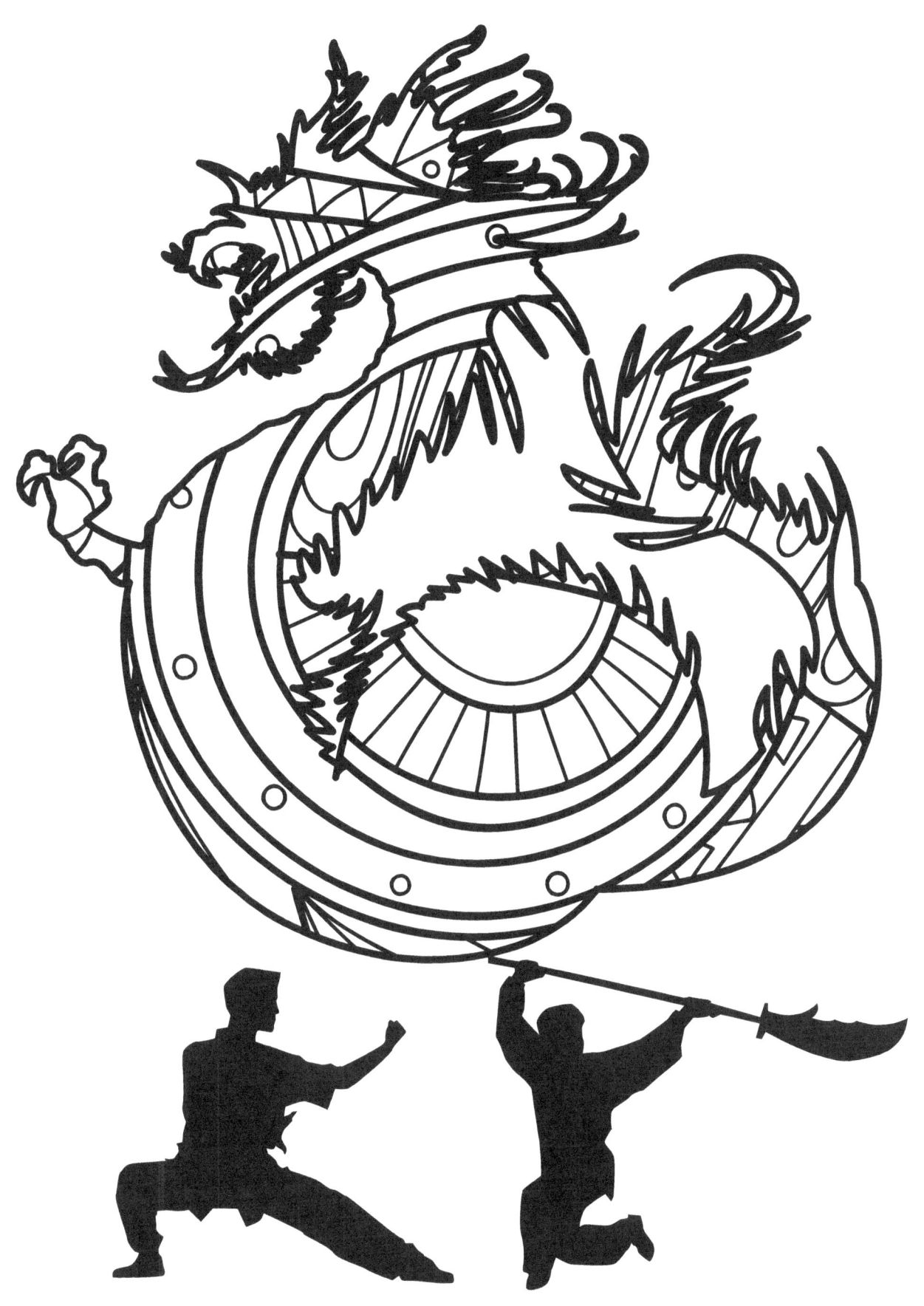

FIGHT THE NINJA DRAGON

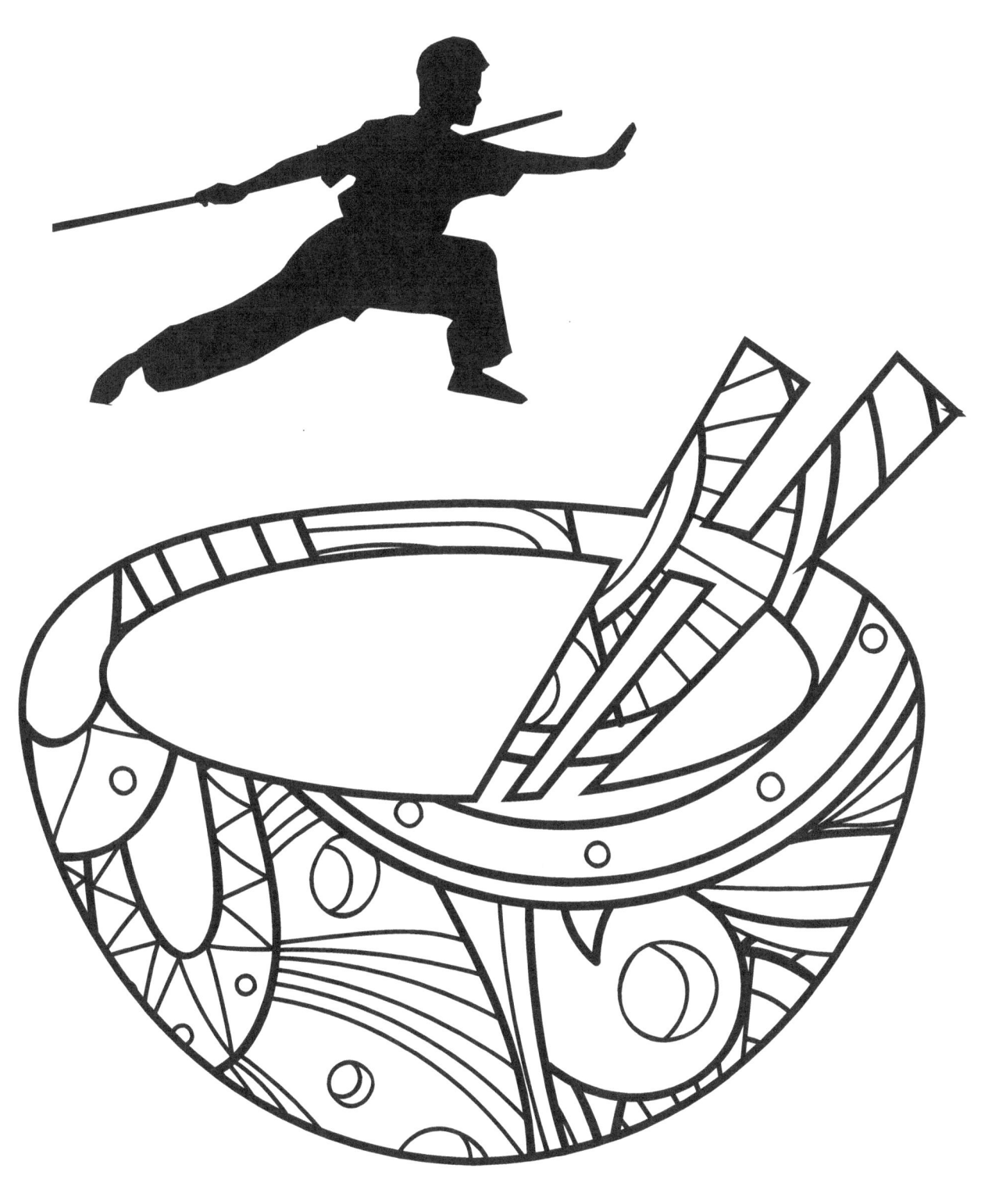

NINJAS EAT TO STAY STRONG

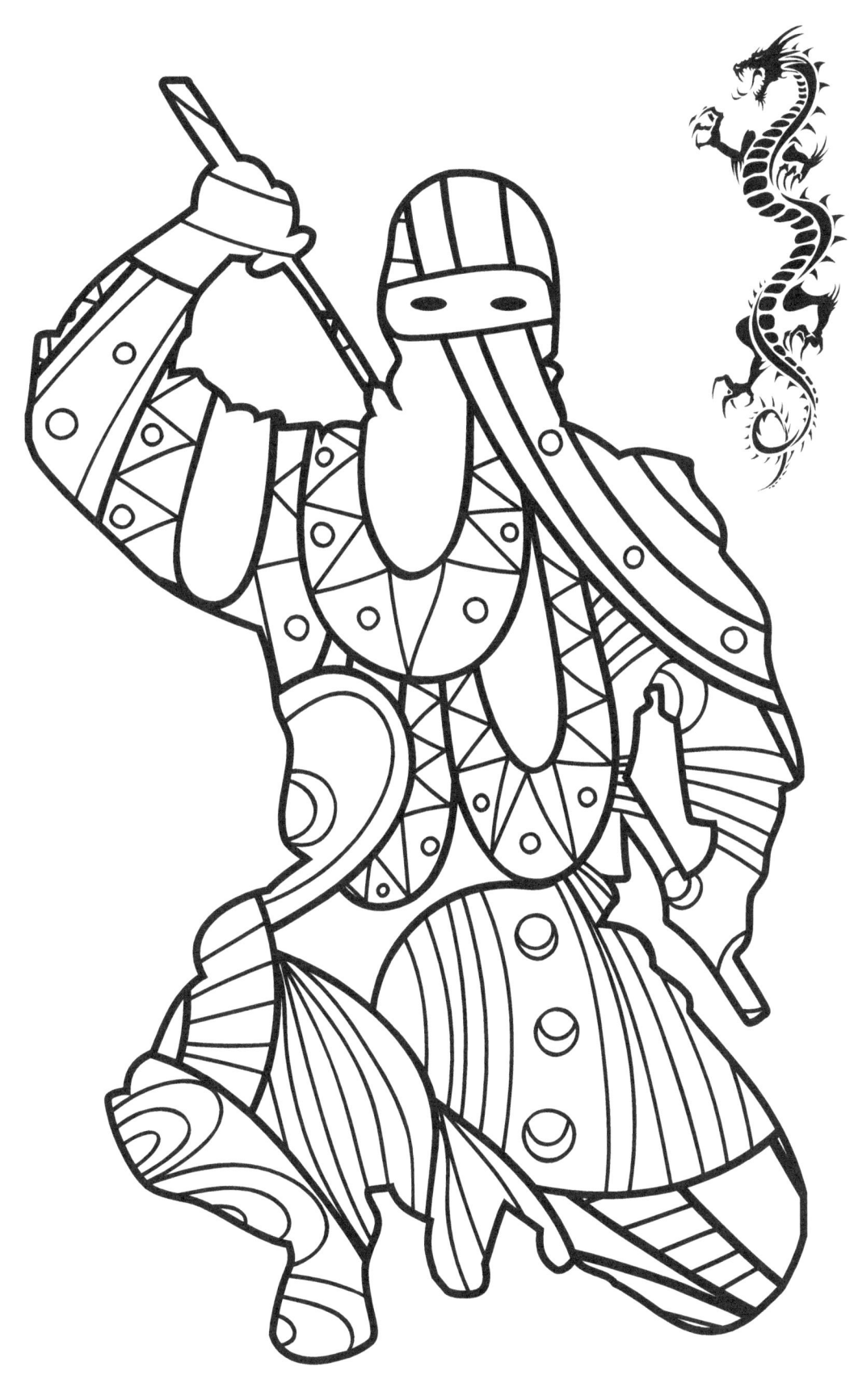

PREPARING FOR NINJA BATTLE

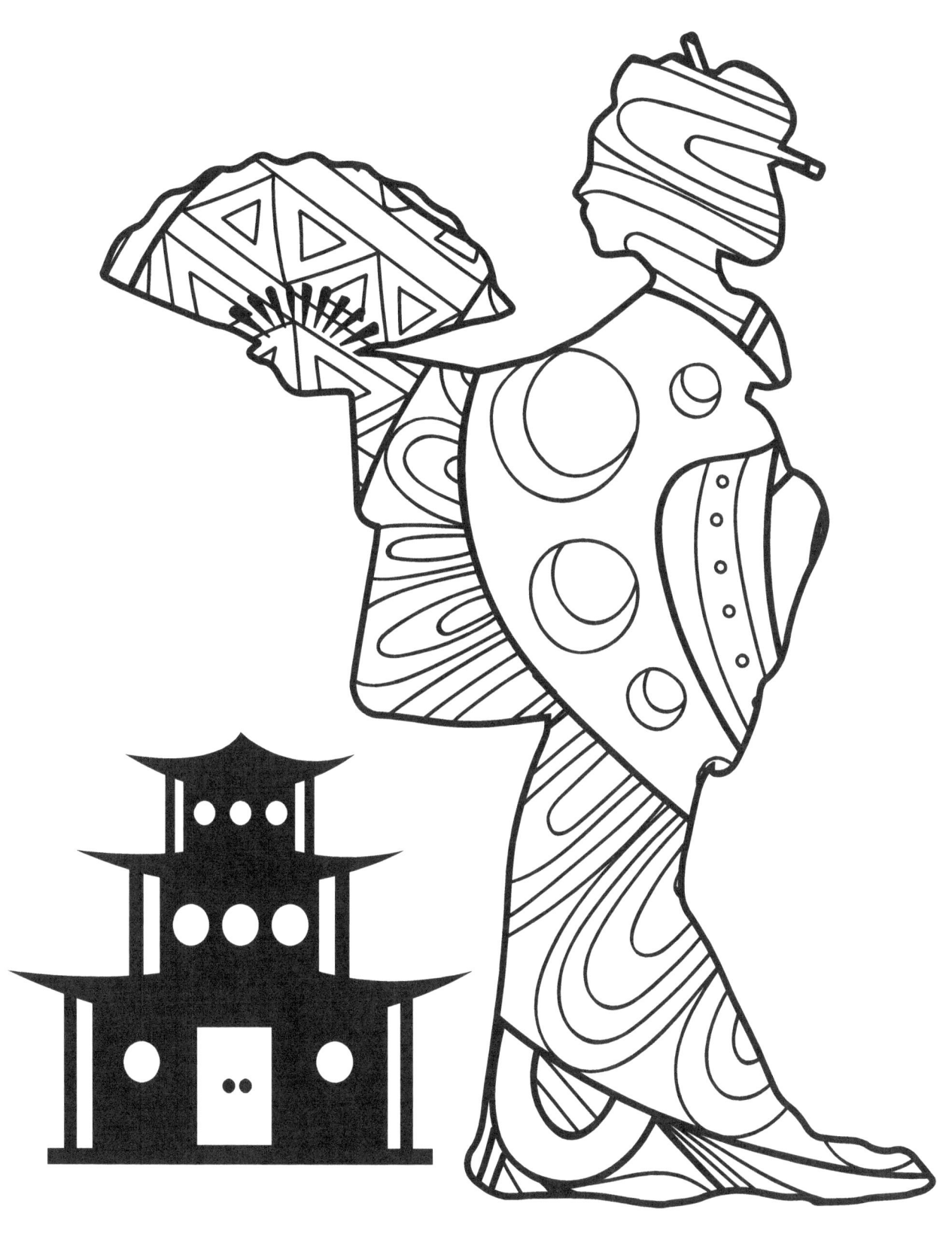

JAPANESE FAN DANCE

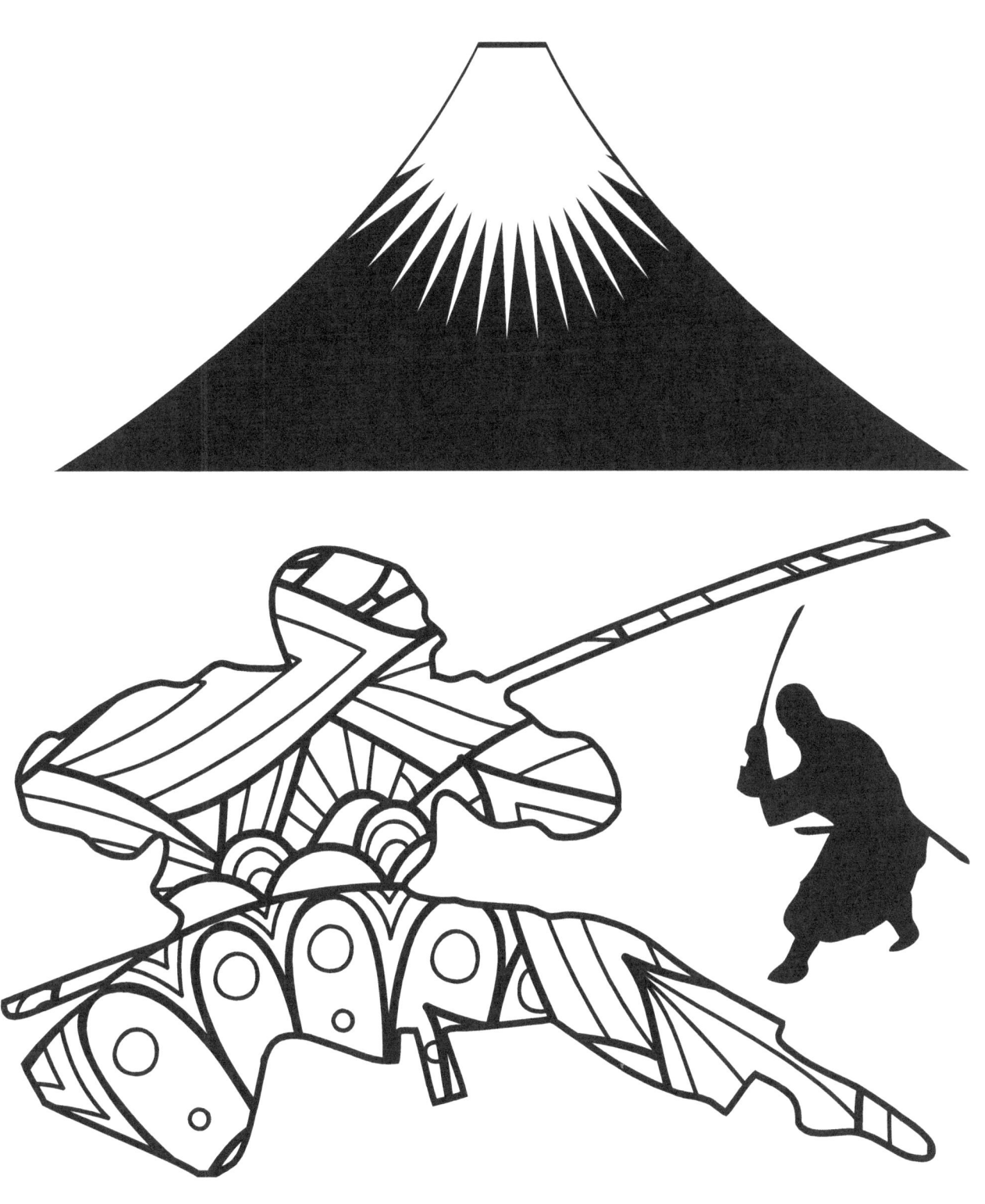

FIGHT AT MOUNT FUJI

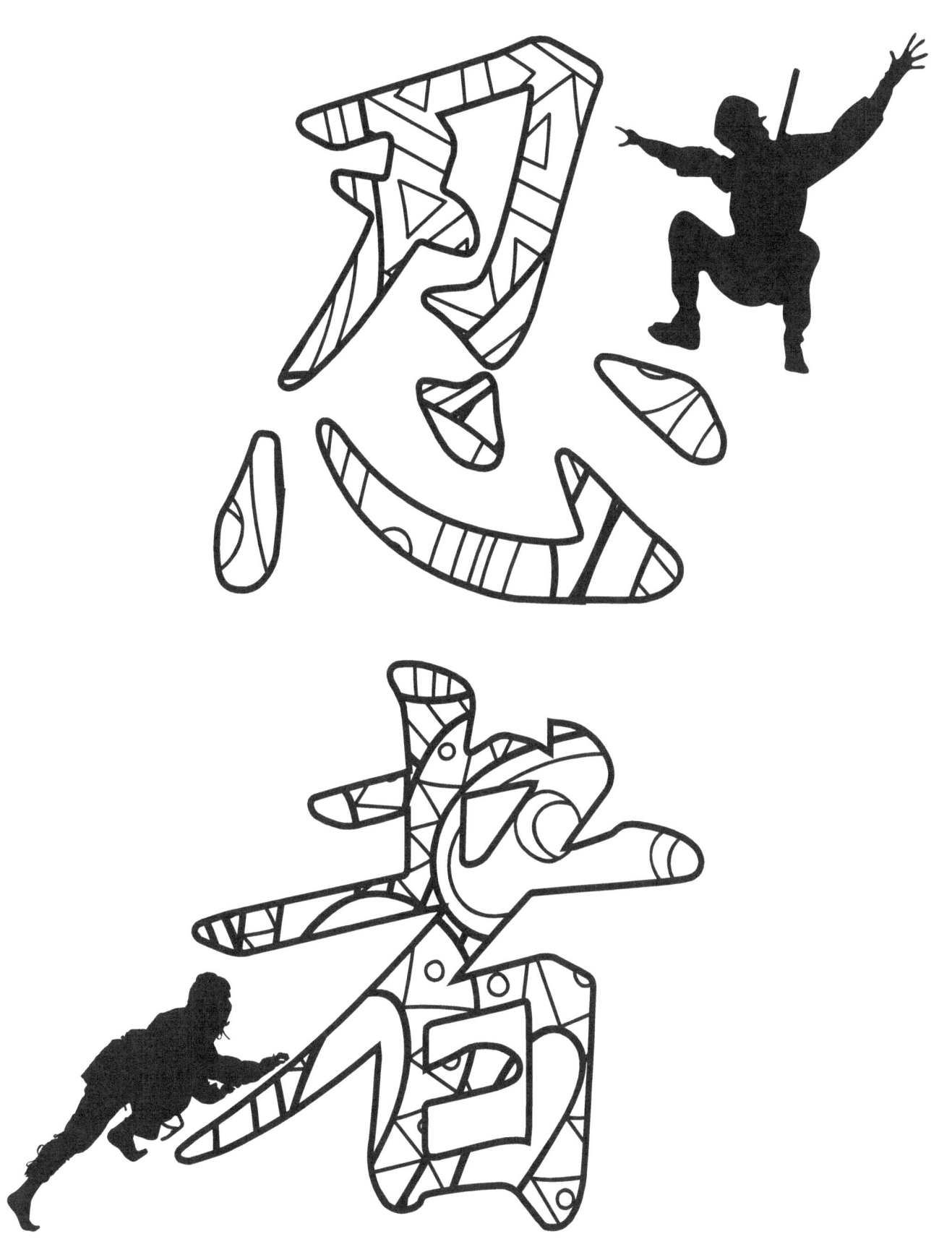

THE JAPANESE SYMBOLS FOR NINJA

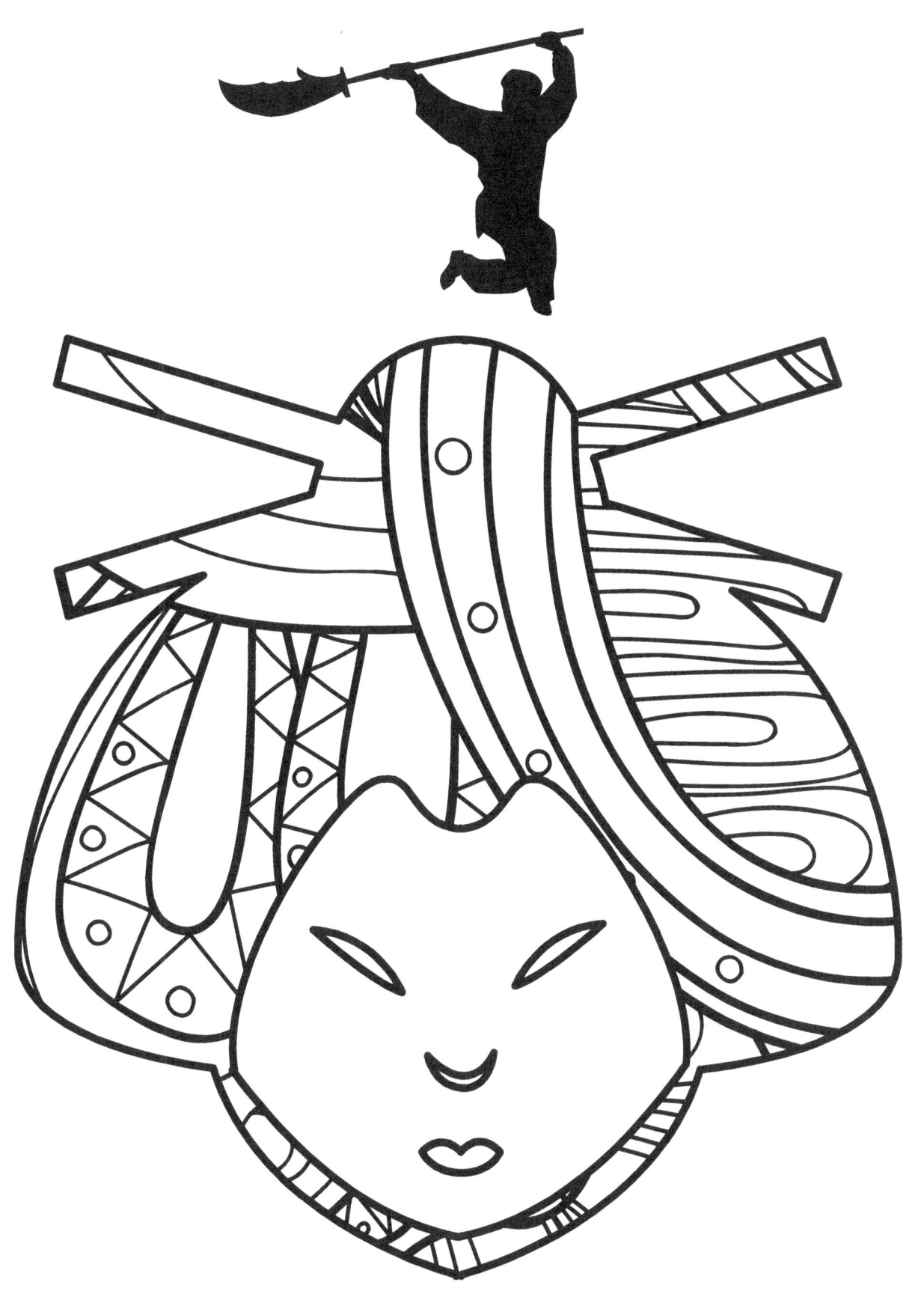

BEAUTIFUL GIRL OR NINJA ASSASSIN?

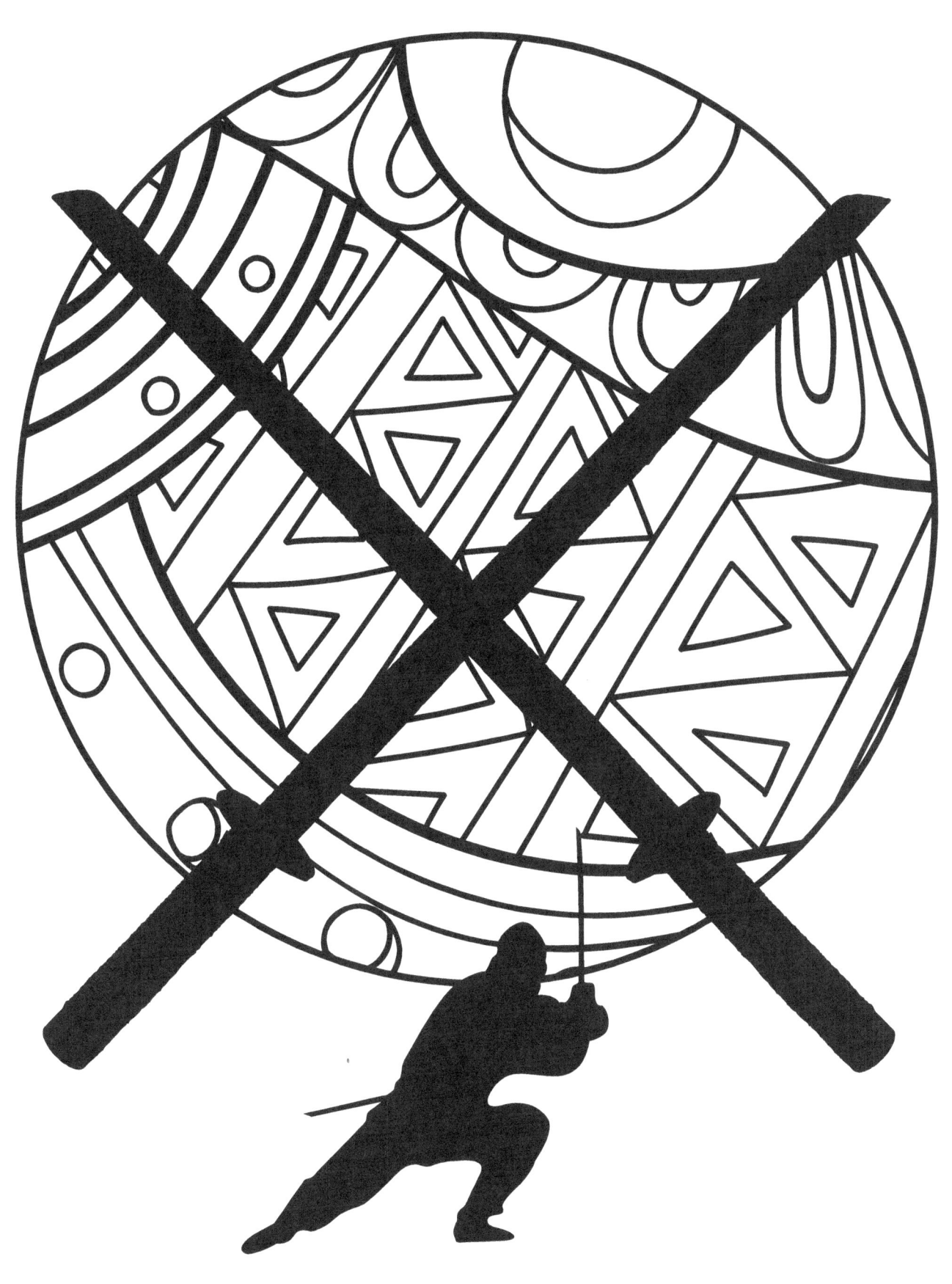

COMBAT NINJA SWORDS